A Guide for Using

Amelia Bedelia

in the Classroom

Based on the novel written by Peggy Parish

This guide written by Mary Bolte

Teacher Created Materials, Inc.
6421 Industry Way
Westminster, CA 92683
www.teachercreated.com
©1997 Teacher Created Materials, Inc.
Reprinted, 2002
Made in U.S.A.
ISBN 1-55734-818-9

Edited by
Candyce Norvell
Walter Kelly

Illustrated by
Howard Chaney

Cover Art by
Sue Fullam

Table of Contents

Introduction and Sample Lessons

Amelia Bedelia is a housekeeper who does things exactly the way the words say. She has been entertaining young readers since 1963 and teaching them that sometimes words have more than one meaning. The 13 books in the series will extend your students' study of the English language while providing many enriching and entertaining experiences. This unit is primarily concerned with the original title, *Amelia Bedelia*. However, we hope you will also share the other titles with your class. The appendix suggests activities for each book in the series. The generic resources beginning on page 41 can be used with any of the books.

A Sample Lesson Plan

The sample lessons on page 4 provide you with a specific set of lesson plan suggestions. Each of the lessons can take from one to several days to complete and can include all or some of the suggested activities. Refer to the Suggestions for Using the Unit Activities on pages 7–10 for information relating to unit activities.

A Unit Planner

If you wish to tailor the suggestions on pages 7–10 to a format other than that prescribed in the Sample Lesson Plan, a blank unit planner is provided on page 5. On a specific day you may choose the activities you wish to include by writing the activity number or a brief notation about the lesson in the "Unit Activities" section. Space has been provided for reminders, comments, and other pertinent information relating to each day's activities. Reproduce copies of the Unit Planner as needed.

Sample Lesson Plan

Lesson 1

- Read page 6 with students to learn about the author and the Amelia Bedelia books.

- Do Before the Book activity 7 on page 7.

- Discuss the Before the Book questions in activity 4 on page 7.

- Read the story for enjoyment.

Lesson 2

- Introduce the vocabulary on page 8.

- Reread the story, listening for the vocabulary words.

- Discuss the seven idioms used in the book.

- Complete Into the Book activity 1 on page 7.

- Complete the time line on page 26.

- Complete the riddle activity on page 18.

Lesson 3

- Complete the pocket chart activity using Bloom's Taxonomy on page 12.

- Discuss the use of "un" at the beginning of a word.

- Discuss the "un" words. Refer to the master list on page 44.

- Complete the "un" words worksheet on page 19.

- Dress the chicken and trim the steak on page 38.

Lesson 4

- Prepare the story sentence strips in Pocket Chart Activity 5 on page 8 and retell the story in sequence.

- Learn about rice. Read and complete the worksheet on page 31.

- Complete the map activity on pages 35 and 36.

- Do the rice experiments on pages 32 and 33.

- Write a letter to Amelia Bedelia on page 20.

- Complete the math worksheet about pie on page 27.

Lesson 5

- Work in groups to make the stick puppet theaters and stick puppets on pages 15–17.

- In groups, practice the reader's theater script on pages 24 and 25.

- Complete the activity on symmetrical shapes on page 28.

- Write a song about Amelia Bedelia on page 40.

- Complete the idiom word search on page 21.

Lesson 6

- Perform the reader's theater for an audience.

- Sing and share the songs about Amelia Bedelia.

Unit Planner

Unit Activities

Date ⬭

Notes/Comments:

Unit Activities

Date ⬭

Notes/Comments:

Unit Activities

Date ⬭

Notes/Comments:

Unit Activities

Date ⬭

Notes/Comments:

Unit Activities

Date ⬭

Notes/Comments:

Unit Activities

Date ⬭

Notes/Comments:

Getting to Know the Book and Author

About the Book

Amelia Bedelia is published by Harper Collins, available in Canada and UK from Harper Collins Publishers and in AUS from Harper Collins.

Have you ever dusted the furniture or changed the towels in the bathroom or put out the lights when you were finished in the living room? These are some of the easy jobs that Amelia Bedelia, as a new maid, is supposed to do for Mr. and Mrs. Rogers after they leave for the day. But Amelia Bedelia takes her directions literally. She does dust the furniture . . . smothering it with scented dusting powder. She does change the towels . . . using scissors to snip them into new shapes. She does put out the lights . . . clipping the light bulbs with clothespins to the outdoor clothesline.

These are just a few of the jobs that Amelia Bedelia does on her first day with the Rogers. Upon their return, the Rogers are puzzled and upset. But when they taste the lemon-meringue pie Amelia has baked, they decide she must stay . . . and she does.

Each moment provides a silly experience with idioms and homonyms that spark the reader's interest.

About the Author

Children were always a part of Peggy Parish's life, so writing children's stories came naturally. The author of more than 40 books for children was born in 1927 in Manning, South Carolina. She was educated at the University of South Carolina and received a B.A. in English. Later she did graduate study at George Peabody College for Teachers, which is now Vanderbilt University. Peggy was an elementary teacher for 15 years and received many awards and honors for her books.

Peggy once mentioned that the things she had Amelia do must appear to be true. When she wrote *Good Work, Amelia Bedelia,* she thought of having her make a sponge cake in the literal way. So one afternoon Peggy spent time in the kitchen snipping pieces of sponge into cake batter. The sponge did not change during the baking process, and that was the way she wrote it in her book.

Peggy Parish

Peggy Parish died on November 19, 1988. Her nephew, Herman Parish, has continued where his aunt left off. He was in the fourth grade when Peggy Parish wrote her first book about Amelia Bedelia. In 1995, Herman Parish's book, *Good Driving, Amelia Bedelia,* was published, continuing Amelia's adventures.

Suggestions for Using the Unit Activities

Use some or all of the following suggestions to introduce students to *Amelia Bedelia* and to extend their appreciation of the book through activities that cross the curriculum. The suggested activities have been divided into three sections to assist the teacher in planning the literature unit.

The suggestions are in the following sections:

- *Before the Book:* suggestions for preparing the classroom environment and the students for the literature to be read
- *Into the Book:* activities that focus on the book's content, characters, theme, etc.
- *After the Book:* extends the reader's enjoyment and links with other Amelia Bedelia books

Before the Book

1. Before you begin the unit, prepare the vocabulary cards, story questions, and sentence strips for the pocket chart activities. (See page 8 [activity 4], page 12, and page 14.)

2. Explain to students that there are 13 Amelia Bedelia books. (Display the books in the series.) Also call attention to the newest book of the series, *Good Driving, Amelia Bedelia*, written by Peggy Parish's nephew, Herman Parish. The first book you will be reading is *Amelia Bedelia,* published in 1963.

3. Read about the author (page 6) to learn more about Peggy Parish.

4. Build background and set the stage discussing the students' responses to these questions:

   What are maids and housekeepers? Why do people hire them? What kind of work do they do? Where do they usually work?

5. Display the cover of the book. What does it tell you about Amelia Bedelia? What kind of clothes is she wearing? Why do people wear uniforms? What are different kinds of uniforms that people wear? What do you think Amelia is doing?

6. Introduce the other two characters in the book, Mr. and Mrs. Rogers. Note that the Rogers appear in all the books.

7. Familiarize students with the term *idiom.* Idioms are expressions that have nonliteral meanings. They don't mean exactly what they say. Refer to the master list of idioms on pages 42 and 43 to assist students in learning this term.

Into the Book

1. Idioms

Write the idioms used in the book on large light bulbs made of construction paper. If possible, display these bulbs on a clothesline across the room.

- Change the towels in the green bathroom.
- Dust the furniture.
- Draw the drapes when the sun comes in.
- Put the lights out when you finish in the living room.
- Measure two cups of rice.
- Trim the fat on the steak.
- Dress the chicken.

Suggestions for Using the Unit Activities *(cont.)*

1. **Idioms** (cont.)

   After reading the book the first time, have students choose one of the seven idioms and draw it as Amelia performed it. Enlarge the light bulb shape on page 13 and have students make their drawings on copies of it.

2. **Pocket Chart Activities: Story Questions**

   Develop critical thinking skills with the story questions on page 14. The questions are based on Bloom's Taxonomy and are provided in each of Bloom's Levels of Learning. Reproduce copies of the pie pattern on page 13 and write a story question on each pie.

3. **Pocket Chart Activities: Vocabulary Cards**

   Discuss the meanings of the following words and phrases in context after reading the book. Make copies of the light bulbs on page 13. Write the words on the light bulbs. Display the bulbs in a pocket chart. (See page 11.)

grand house	icebox	drapes
maid/housekeeper	dusting powder	measure
lemon-meringue pie	undust	container
rich folks	unlight	fade

4. **Pocket Chart Activities: Riddles, Sentences, Quotations, Idioms**

   - Write riddles for the three characters: Amelia Bedelia, Mr. Rogers, and Mrs. Rogers. Display them in the pocket chart with student-drawn pictures for a matching game.

   - Brainstorm a list of sentences retelling important events from the story. Display them in the pocket chart.

   - Have students put the sentences in the order in which the events happened in the story.

   - Use the sentences to retell the story.

   - Divide the class into small groups and distribute a few sentence strips to each group. Ask the groups to act out the part of the story the sentences describe.

   - Put some quotations from the story on sentence strips. Print the name of each speaker on a separate card. Use them for a matching activity in the pocket chart.

   - Make a list of idioms from the story. Display them in order in the pocket chart.

8

Suggestions for Using the Unit Activities *(cont.)*

5. Language Arts

- *Draw and Undraw the Drapes (page 18)*

  Brainstorm ideas for riddles. Follow the directions. Be sure to cut only on the bold, solid lines and fold back on the dotted lines to form a flap.

- *The "un" Words (page 19)*

  Discuss the meaning of "prefix" and the use of "un" at the beginning of a word. Review the words in the Word Box before beginning the activity. Extend the lesson by researching other prefixes.

- *Write a Letter to Amelia Bedelia (page 20)*

  Review the five parts of a letter and the five geometric shapes on the strips. Students can exchange letters with one another and write return letters as Amelia Bedelia might reply.

- *Amelia's Favorite Word Search (page 21)*

  Before giving the word search to students, discuss the 10 idioms and their meanings. Then, independently, have students complete the puzzle.

- *Now You're the Cook! (page 22)*

  Discuss Amelia Bedelia's special foods and their preparation. Then have students share their favorite foods. Send home the recipe form to be completed. Compile recipes into a class cookbook.

- *Amelia and Alcolu Acrostics (page 23)*

  Explain acrostics. Then have students write acrostics using their names. Discuss cousins, Amelia and Cousin Alcolu. Complete the activity.

- *Reader's Theater Script (pages 24 and 25)*

  Provide a copy of the script for each performer. You may wish to highlight the parts and laminate the scripts before distribution. In groups, students can choose or be assigned parts. Practice reading the script together. When ready to present to an audience, have students stand in a line or semicircle to perform. See page 25 for variations.

6. Math

- *A Time Line for Amelia Bedelia (page 26)*

  Discuss order and ordinal numbers. Review the seven idioms on page 7 and display them in order on the pocket chart. Explain a time line. Then have students complete the activity.

- *Pie! Pie! Pie! (page 27)*

  Brainstorm different kinds of pies and recognize the pies in the code. Have students complete the activity and then write their own code problems using the pie code.

- *Symmetrical Shapes in the Rogers' House (page 28)*

  Plan activities in symmetry. Have the students complete the towel, pie, chicken, light bulb, steak, and drapes on the worksheet.

- *Fraction Pie (page 29)*

  Provide fraction activities with halves, thirds, fourths, fifths, sixths, and eighths. Complete the activity as a class. Discuss other instances where one would use fractions when sharing food.

Suggestions for Using the Unit Activities *(cont.)*

6. Math (cont.)

- *Telephone Tricks (page 30)*

  Examine a telephone with the class. Discuss the placement of numbers and letters on the buttons. Explain that # and * are used for special telephoning services. Have students learn their own telephone numbers. Then complete the activity together or independently.

7. Science/Health

- *Rice Facts (page 31)*

  Read and discuss the rice facts. Label the drawing of the rice plant. Refer to related books in the bibliography.

- *Experiments with Rice (page 32)*

  Do both experiments and record procedure on the Experiment Form on page 33.

- *Science Fun with Amelia Bedelia (page 33)*

  Use this form with all experiments.

- *Likes and Dislikes (page 34)*

  Discuss foods eaten by the Rogers. What were their favorites? What did they dislike? Did they raise any foods? Complete the lunch tray activity.

8. Social Studies

- *Rice and the World (page 35)* and *World Map (page 36)*

  Provide map activities and discuss the cardinal directions. Complete page 35 as a class.

- *Looking for a Job (page 37)*

  Discuss different jobs and qualifications. Review information required and complete the form.

9. Art

- *Dress the Chicken and Trim the Steak (page 38)*

  Discuss Amelia's way and the right way to prepare these meats. Then have students decorate the meat artistically.

- *A New Uniform for Amelia Bedelia (page 39)*

  Brainstorm jobs that require uniforms and why they require them. If possible, display uniforms worn by family and friends. Then have students create a new uniform for Amelia Bedelia.

After the Book

1. Music

- *Write a Song About Amelia Bedelia (page 40)*

  Sing "Old MacDonald Had a Farm." List places that Amelia might work, what she might do there, and words or sounds she might make while working there. Write verses using the format on this page.

2. Generic Resources

- *Idiom Web (page 41)*

  Use this worksheet to web idioms used in other Amelia Bedelia books.

- *Master List of Idioms (pages 42 and 43)*

  Use this list to create your own activities or use with the activities mentioned in this book.

- *Master Lists of "un" Words and Homonyms (page 44)*

  Use these lists to create your own activities or use with the activities mentioned in this book.

Pocket Chart Activities

Prepare a pocket chart for storing and using the vocabulary cards, the story question cards, and the sentence strips.

How to Make a Pocket Chart

If a commercial pocket chart is unavailable, you can make a pocket chart if you have access to a laminator. Begin by laminating a 24" x 36" (60 cm x 90 cm) piece of colored tagboard. Run about 20" (50 cm) of additional plastic. To make nine pockets, cut the clear plastic into nine equal strips. Space the strips equally down the 36" (90 cm) length of the tagboard. Attach each strip with cellophane tape along the bottom and sides. This will hold the sentence strips, word cards, etc., and can be displayed in a learning center or mounted on a chalk tray for use with a group. When your pocket chart is ready, use it to display sentence strips, vocabulary words, and question cards. A sample chart is provided below.

How to Use a Pocket Chart

1. On white or colored construction or index paper, reproduce the light bulb pattern on page 13. Make vocabulary cards as directed on page 8. Print the definitions on sentence strips for a matching activity.

2. Select idioms from the stories and print them on sentence strips. Match the idioms to their meanings.

3. Select homonyms, idioms, or "un" words from the master lists and print them on sentence strips. Match them to their meanings.

Pocket Chart Activities *(cont.)*

4. Print events from the story on sentence strips. Have students display them in sequential order.

5. Reproduce several copies of the pie pattern (page 13) on six different colors of construction paper. Use a different paper color to represent each of Bloom's Levels of Learning.

Example:

    I. Knowledge *(pink)*

    II. Comprehension *(yellow)*

    III. Application *(orange)*

    IV. Analysis *(light green)*

    V. Synthesis *(tan)*

    VI. Evaluation *(white)*

Write a story question from page 14 on the appropriate color-coded pie. Write the level of the question and the question on the front of the pie as shown in the example above.

• Use the pie-shaped cards after reading the story to provide opportunities for students to develop and practice higher-level critical thinking skills. Using the color coding system, you may choose to question the students at one level or you may choose to use all of the levels. The cards can be used with some or all of the following activities.

• Have a student choose a card and read it aloud or give it to the teacher to read aloud. Have the student answer the question or call on a volunteer to answer it.

• Pair students. Read a question and have partners take turns answering.

• Play a game. Divide the class into teams. Ask for a response to a question written on one of the cards. Score a point for each appropriate response. If question cards have been prepared for several different Amelia Bedelia books, mix up the cards and ask team members to respond by naming the book that relates to the question. Extra points can be awarded if a team member answers the question correctly.

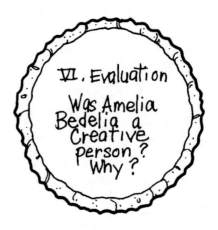

Pocket Chart Patterns

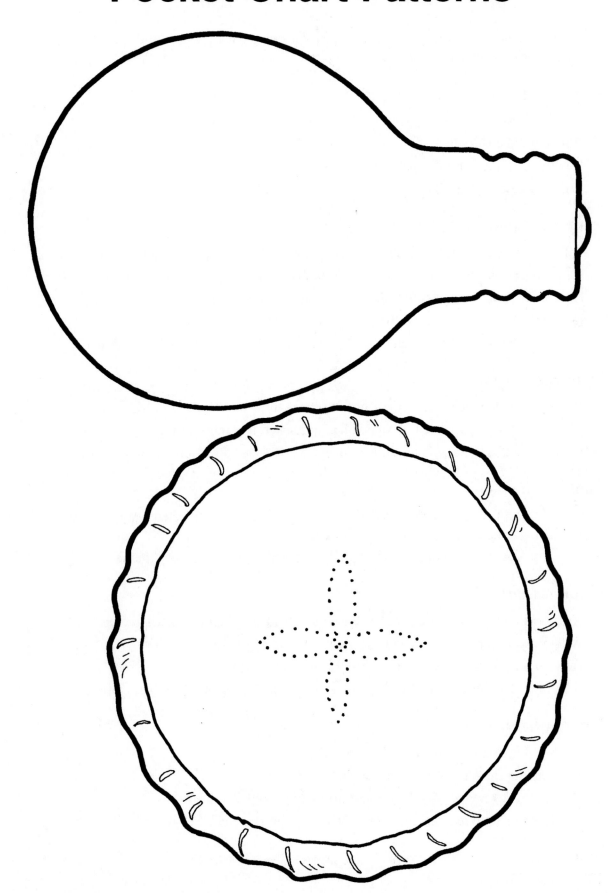

Story Questions

Use the following questions with the suggested activities on page 12. Prepare the pie patterns (page 13) and write a different question on each pie.

I. Knowledge *(pink)*

- Who were Mr. and Mrs. Rogers?
- Where did the story take place?
- What were the seven jobs that Mrs. Rogers wanted Amelia to do?
- What was the surprise that Amelia made for the Rogers?

II. Comprehension *(yellow)*

- Tell why Amelia Bedelia wanted to bake a lemon-meringue pie for the Rogers.
- Mrs. Rogers told Amelia to do just what the list said. Do you think she did? Why?
- Do you think Mr. and Mrs. Rogers were happy with Amelia's work? Why?
- How did Mrs. Rogers change the way she explained her job list?
- Explain what happened that changed Mr. and Mrs. Rogers' feelings about Amelia.

III. Application *(orange)*

- If Amelia Bedelia had performed her jobs correctly, what might have happened?
- What might have happened if Amelia had not baked a lemon-meringue pie?
- Do you think Amelia will continue to take Mrs. Rogers' directions literally? Why?

IV. Analysis *(light green)*

- What jobs did Amelia perform differently than Mrs. Rogers expected? Why do you think the pie changed the Rogers' feelings about Amelia?
- How did Mrs. Rogers change the wording of her new directions for Amelia?

V. Synthesis *(tan)*

- How would this story have ended if the Rogers had hated lemon-meringue pie?
- What do you think would have happened if Mr. and Mrs. Rogers had stayed home?
- How could the story have been different if the house had been computerized?
- If children had lived in the Rogers' house, how could the story have been different?

VI. Evaluation *(white)*

- Do you think Amelia enjoyed her job? Why?
- Was Amelia Bedelia a creative person? Why?
- Do you think Mr. and Mrs. Rogers are forgiving people? Why?
- Would you like to read another book about Amelia Bedelia? Why?

Stick Puppet Theaters

Make a class set of puppet theaters (one for each student) or make one theater for every two to four students.

Materials: 22" x 28" (56 cm x 71 cm) pieces of colored poster board (enough for each student or group of students); markers, crayons, or paints; scissors or craft knife

Directions:

1. Fold the poster board about 8" (20 cm) in from each of the shorter sides.
2. In the center of the theater, cut a "window" large enough to accommodate two or three puppets. (See illustration.)
3. Let students personalize and decorate their own theaters.
4. Laminate the theaters to make them more durable. You may wish to send the theaters home at the end of the year or save them to use year after year.

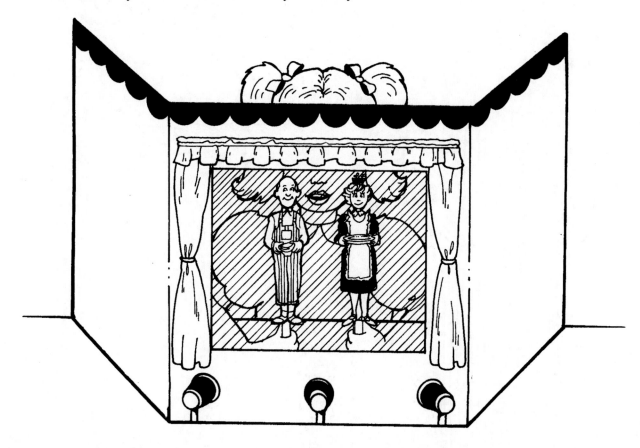

Suggestions for Using the Puppets and the Puppet Theaters:

1. Prepare the stick puppets using the directions on page 16. Use the puppets and the puppet theaters with the reader's theater script on pages 24 and 25. (Let small groups of students take turns reading the parts and using the stick puppets.)
2. Let students experiment with the puppets by telling the story in their own words.
3. Read quotations from the book or make statements about the characters and ask students to hold up the stick puppets represented by the quotes or statements.

Stick Puppet Patterns

Directions: Reproduce the patterns on tagboard or construction paper. Color the patterns. Cut along the dotted lines. To complete the stick puppets, glue each pattern to a tongue depressor or craft stick. Use the puppets with puppet theaters and/or the reader's theater script.

Stick Puppet Patterns *(cont.)*

See page 16 for directions.

Name _____

Draw and Undraw the Drapes

Guess Who? What? Why? Where? or When?

Write a riddle about the book on each set of drapes. Cut on the solid black lines. Fold back each set of drapes on the dotted lines. Glue, or staple this paper to another sheet the same size or larger. (**Note:** Keep drape flaps folded back so that you do not glue or staple the flaps to the bottom sheet of paper.) Then write the answer on the inside. Decorate your drapes and share with a friend. Draw (close) the drapes to read the riddle. Undraw (open) the drapes to find the answer!

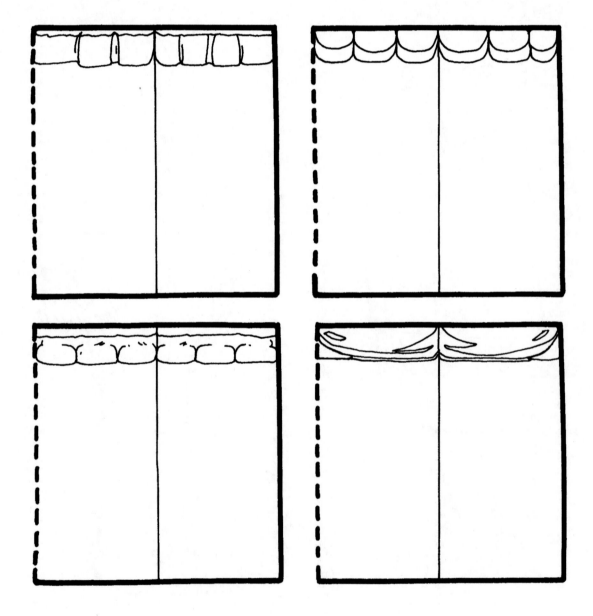

Name _____

The "un" Words

A *prefix* is a syllable that is put at the beginning of a word to change its meaning. "Un" is a prefix that means "the opposite of."

Mrs. Rogers learned to put "un" in front of words so Amelia Bedelia could understand their meanings. Choose five "un" words from the word box and use each word in a sentence.

Word Box			
unbutton	unfold	unfriendly	unroll
unhappy	unhook	unlock	unripe
unbuckle	uncover	unlucky	unsafe

1. _____

_____

2. _____

_____

3. _____

_____

4. _____

_____

5. _____

_____

Now choose one of your sentences and draw a picture on the other side of this paper. Share it with a friend.

Write a Letter to Amelia Bedelia

Amelia Bedelia changed the shapes of the towels in the green bathroom. Maybe she snipped them into circles, squares, stars, triangles, or diamonds. Cut out the five rectangles at the bottom of the page. Then paste each one on the dotted line next to the matching part of a letter. Finally, write a letter to Amelia Bedelia.

☐ _____   _____

_____   _____ ○

☆

△ _____   _____

◇ _____   _____

- -

| ○ **Greeting** | ☐ **Date** | ☆ **Message** |

| △ **Closing** | ◇ **Signature** |

Name _____

Amelia's Favorite Word Search

In the list below, find the word that is missing from each idiom. Write it on the line. Then look for the word in the word search puzzle. The words may go up, down, across, or on a diagonal. Circle each word when you find it.

1. The early bird catches the_____.

2. Don't _____ me!

3. Hold your _____!

4. You have a _____ thumb.

5. That's a piece of_____.

6. I'm going_____!

7. That went in one _____ and out the other.

8. I'm in a _____!

9. That's for the _____!

10. I'm sitting on top of the _____!

Word List

world

green

worm

ear

bug

pickle

horses

cake

bananas

birds

B	A	N	A	N	A	S	Z	B
F	M	R	V	Z	D	E	O	U
I	S	U	Y	H	L	S	T	G
W	O	R	M	K	Q	N	K	S
O	G	N	C	P	E	C	D	A
R	A	I	O	E	J	R	C	U
L	P	J	R	T	I	E	A	R
D	R	G	M	B	X	L	K	T
W	K	C	H	O	R	S	E	S

Name _____

Now You're the Cook!

Amelia Bedelia loved to cook. Share your favorite recipe. Complete the recipe form and return it to school.

Ingredients:_____

_____

_____

_____

_____

_____

_____

_____

Directions:_____

_____

_____

_____

_____

_____

_____

Cook:_____

Amelia and Alcolu Acrostics

An *acrostic* is a poem in which the first letters of each line, taken in order, spell a word.

Amelia and Cousin Alcolu have fun together and help each other. Complete these acrostics using their names. The first lines are done for you.

Amelia has a cousin named Alcolu.

M _____

E _____

L _____

I _____

A _____

Alcolu has a cousin named Amelia.

L _____

C _____

O _____

L _____

U _____

Reader's Theater Script

Characters		
Narrator 1	**Narrator 3**	**Mrs. Rogers**
Narrator 2	**Amelia Bedelia**	**Mr. Rogers**

Mrs. Rogers:	I have made a list of your jobs, since I will be gone on your first day of work. Mr. Rogers and I will be back later. Bye!
Amelia Bedelia:	I really like them and am happy to work here. They live in such a big house! They must be rich.
Narrator 1:	Since Amelia Bedelia baked good pies, she decided to surprise the Rogers and make a lemon-meringue pie.
Narrator 2:	She made the pie and put it into the oven. Then she began reading the list.
Amelia Bedelia:	The first job on the list says to change the towels in the green bathroom. They look so good, I wonder why they need to be changed.
Narrator 3:	She knew she should do what the list told her, so she got some scissors and cut and changed those towels.
Amelia Bedelia:	The second job on the list says to dust the furniture. I would rather undust the furniture. Oh well, I must do what the list says.
Narrator 1:	She took a box with "Dusting Powder" written on it and dusted the furniture.
Amelia Bedelia:	The furniture smells great with all the powder dusted on it! Now let's see what's third on the list. When the sun comes in, draw the drapes. I'm not very good at drawing, but I'll try.
Narrator 2:	Amelia sat down and had fun drawing the drapes. Then she read her fourth job.
Amelia Bedelia:	When you're finished in the living room, put out the lights. I'll just unscrew these bulbs and hang them on the clothesline! Oh! I'd better check my pie!
Narrator 3:	In the kitchen, Amelia took the pie out of the oven to cool and then read her fifth job.
Amelia Bedelia:	This says I am supposed to measure two cups of rice. This will be easy with my tape measure . . . just 4 ½ inches! This is really a funny job!
Narrator 1:	She poured the rice back into the box and read the last two jobs on the list.
Amelia Bedelia:	Before you put the steak in the refrigerator, trim the fat and dress the chicken, too.
Narrator 2:	Amelia had fun decorating the fat with ribbon and lace and dressing up the chicken like a boy. Then she put him in a box. Soon the Rogers returned, and Mr. Rogers rushed in.

Reader's Theater Script *(cont.)*

Mr. Rogers:	Why are all those light bulbs hanging on the clothesline?
Amelia Bedelia:	The list said to put the lights out but not to bring them inside.
Mrs. Rogers:	You should have drawn the drapes because the sun will fade the furniture! And why is this furniture so dusty?
Amelia Bedelia:	I did draw a wonderful picture of the drapes, and I used the dusting powder for your furniture!
Mr. Rogers:	My, how these towels have changed!
Amelia Bedelia:	They really do look different. Do you like them?
Mrs. Rogers:	I am going to cook dinner. Where is the rice you measured?
Amelia Bedelia:	It measured 4 ½ inches, but I put it back into the box.
Mrs. Rogers:	I'll get the steak and the chicken out of the refrigerator. Why is this steak covered with ribbon and lace? Why is this chicken dressed in a suit?
Amelia Bedelia:	I think they both look cute. I did what the list said: Trim the fat on the steak and dress the chicken.
Narrator 3:	Mrs. Rogers was really upset and angry. She was about to tell Amelia Bedelia she was fired, when Mr. Rogers stuck something delicious into her mouth.
Mrs. Rogers:	Oh, this lemon-meringue pie is scrumptious!
Amelia Bedelia:	I bake good pies, and I wanted you to have something special!
Narrator 1:	Amelia Bedelia stayed, and Mrs. Rogers learned to write her lists in a different way, using undust instead of dust, close instead of draw, etcetera.
Narrator 2:	Mr. Rogers was mostly interested in Amelia's lemon-meringue pie . . . and they both agreed that she would stay forever.

The End

Variations for Performance

- There can be two casts. One reads while the other performs the actions of the characters or manipulates the stick puppets.

- All performers stand with their backs to the audience. When a performer reads his/her lines, he/she turns, faces the audience, and reads the lines. When finished, he/she turns his/her back to the audience again.

- Make masks for the characters.

- Make decorative name tags to identify the readers.

- Create a backdrop and use props, costumes, and music.

A Time Line for Amelia Bedelia

Name _____

Make a time line showing the order of Amelia Bedelia's jobs. First, cut at the dotted line. Then, color the pictures. Last, cut out the pictures and glue them above the ordinal numbers to show the order in which Amelia Bedelia finished her jobs.

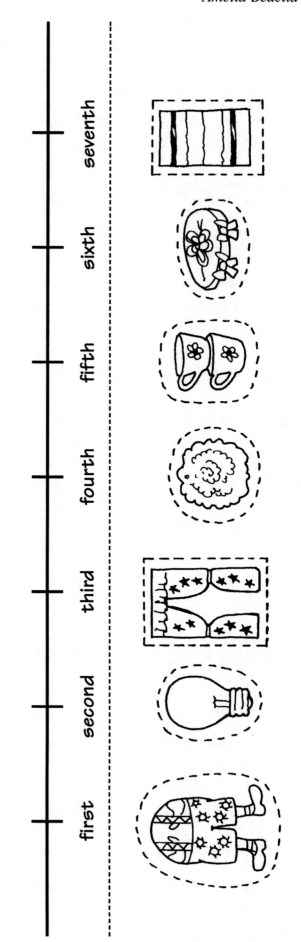

first   second   third   fourth   fifth   sixth   seventh

Name _____

Pie! Pie! Pie!

Use the pie code below. Write a number answer for each problem. When you are finished, write two addition problems and two subtraction problems using the pie code. Use the back of this paper. Exchange with a friend to solve.

1	2	3
+ _____	− _____	+ _____

4	5	6
− _____	+ _____	− _____

7	8	9
+ _____	− _____	+ _____

1 (lime)	2	3	4 (chocolate)	5	6
7	8	9 (peanut butter)	10	11 (blueberry)	12

Name _____

Symmetrical Shapes in the Rogers' House

A shape is symmetrical when the size, shape, and placement of parts on the opposite sides of an imaginary line are exactly the same.

Directions:

Make these shapes symmetrical by finishing the whole shape on the opposite side of the dotted line. When you are finished, write a list of symmetrical shapes that you see in your classroom. Use the back of this paper.

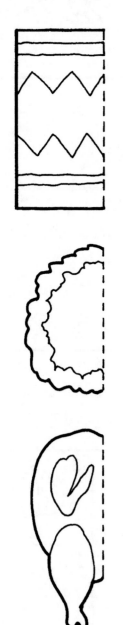

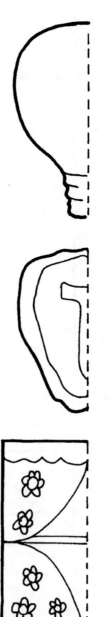

Fraction Pie

Below each pie is the number of people who will share it. Show how you would cut each pie into that number of equal pieces.

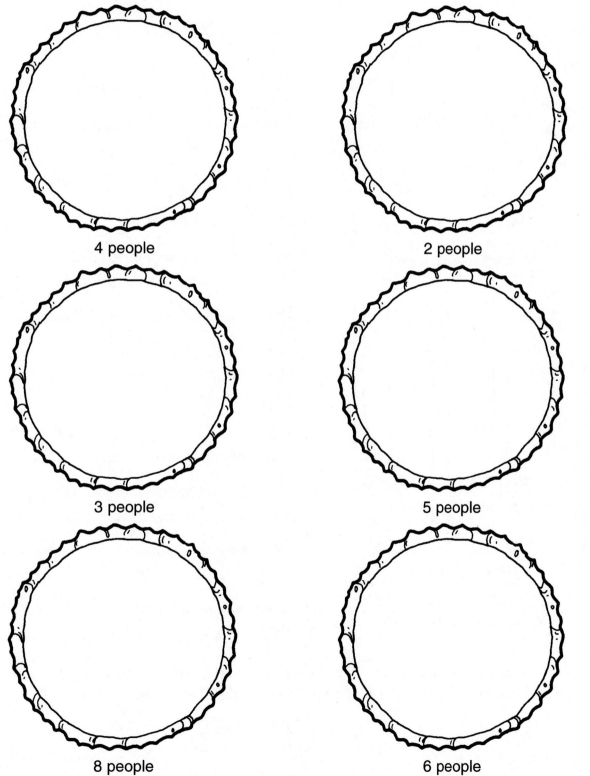

4 people

2 people

3 people

5 people

8 people

6 people

Name _____

Telephone Tricks

As a maid, Amelia Bedelia had to use the telephone a lot. Use this telephone to complete this activity.

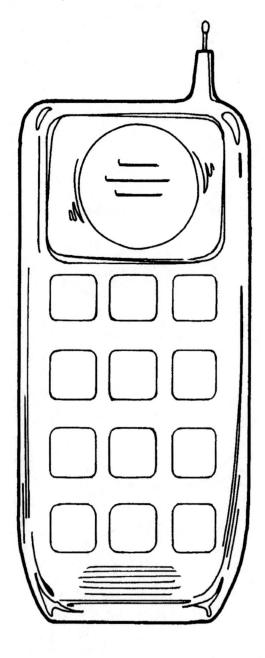

1. How many buttons are there on this telephone?_____

2. Put the numbers 0-9 on the correct buttons.

3. What signs belong on the other buttons? _____ and_____

4. Find out what these 2 buttons mean.

5. Write your area code: _____

6. Now write your telephone number:

   _____

7. How many numbers are in your telephone number? _____

8. Now write your area code in front of your telephone number: _____

9. How many numbers are in your area code plus telephone number? _____

10. Write the odd numbers in your telephone number: _____

11. Write the even numbers in your telephone number: _____

12. Add all the digits in your telephone number. Write the sum._____

13. Make up one addition problem and one subtraction problem using the digits in your telephone number. Write them below or on the back of this paper.

Name _____

Rice Facts

Learn about rice. When you are finished reading, label the parts of a rice plant. New rice words to learn are in boldface.

1. **Rice** is a **grain**.

2. Rice belongs to the **grass family** like wheat, corn, and oats.

3. Rice grows in warm, wet **climates**.

4. Rice grows in fields called **paddies**. The paddies are covered with shallow water. Farmers build low dirt walls called **dikes** or **levees** to hold the water in the paddies.

5. Young rice plants are bright green. They turn golden-yellow as they age.

6. A rice plant grows from 31 to 72 inches (79 cm to 183 cm) tall and usually has three **stems**.

7. Rice is a good source of **carbohydrates** that give the body energy.

8. Rice has little **fat** and is easy to **digest**.

9. The main parts of the rice plants are the **roots**, **stems**, **leaves**, and **panicle**. The panicle holds the **kernels** of rice.

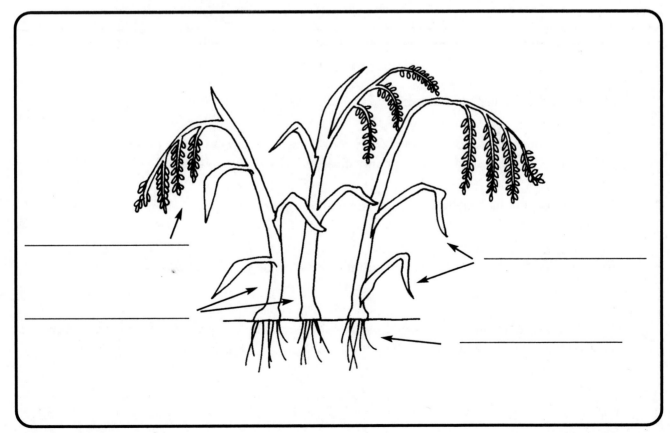

Experiments with Rice

Teacher Information Guide

These experiments may be done by the teacher or by groups of students. Students may complete the Science Fun with Amelia Bedelia form on page 33 as each step is completed.

Experiment 1

Question: What happens to rice when it is boiled? Have students write what they think will happen.

Materials: measuring cup, rice, 2-quart (1.9 L) saucepan with lid, water, hot plate, spoon, and bowls

Experiment: Measure 1 cup (250 mL) of rice. Measure 2 cups (.47 L) of water into a saucepan. Boil the water. Pour in 1 cup (250 mL) of rice. Put the lid on the pot and simmer for 35–45 minutes if using natural rice. For minute rice and other kinds of rice, check the directions on the box.

Results: The rice absorbs the water and expands when boiled. It should occupy twice as much space or more than before it was boiled. It also becomes soft.

Conclusions: Rice expands when it is boiled. This is because of the starch in rice.

Experiment 2

Question: What other foods contain starch?

Materials: tincture of iodine; eyedropper; cookie sheet; different kinds of crackers, cereal, and/or chips; cheese; sugar; bread; potato slice

Experiment: Put the materials to be tested on the cookie sheet. Put 1 drop of iodine on each of the materials.

Results: The foods containing starch will turn a dark blue-purple. The others should show a brown stain.

Conclusions: When iodine is added to starch, a blue-purple compound is formed. Crackers, cereal, chips, bread, and potatoes contain starch.

Name _____

Science Fun with Amelia Bedelia

Question _____

I think_____

_____

_____

Materials I used_____

_____

_____

What I did _____

_____

_____

What happened_____

_____

_____

What I learned _____

_____

_____

_____

Name _____

Likes and Dislikes

Amelia Bedelia likes to bake lemon-meringue pies, and Mr. and Mrs. Rogers like to eat them. What are your favorite foods? What foods do you dislike? Do you grow or raise any kinds of food? Complete the lunch tray with words and pictures.

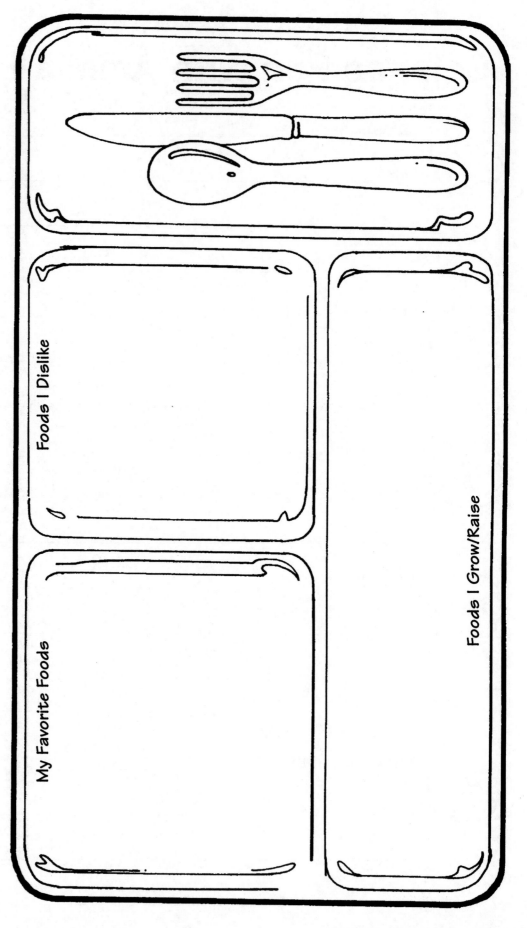

Foods I Dislike

My Favorite Foods

Foods I Grow/Raise

Name _____

Rice and the World

Use the map on page 36 to complete the following activities.

1. Write the four cardinal directions at the bottom below the map.

2. Write the name of the country in which you live._____

   _____Put an X on this country on the map.

3. Write the name of the continent on which you live._____

   _____

4. China and India grow more than half the world's rice. Write an **R** on these two countries.

5. China and India are on the continent of _____.

6. Label the seven continents with the following letters.

   > **a. Africa**   **e. Europe**
   >
   > **b. Antarctica**   **f. North America**
   >
   > **c. Asia**   **g. South America**
   >
   > **d. Australia**

7. Look at the things in your desk. See if they have labels showing the country in which they were made. Write the names of those countries on the line below. See if you can find those countries on the map.

   _____

   _____

   _____

   _____

   _____

World Map

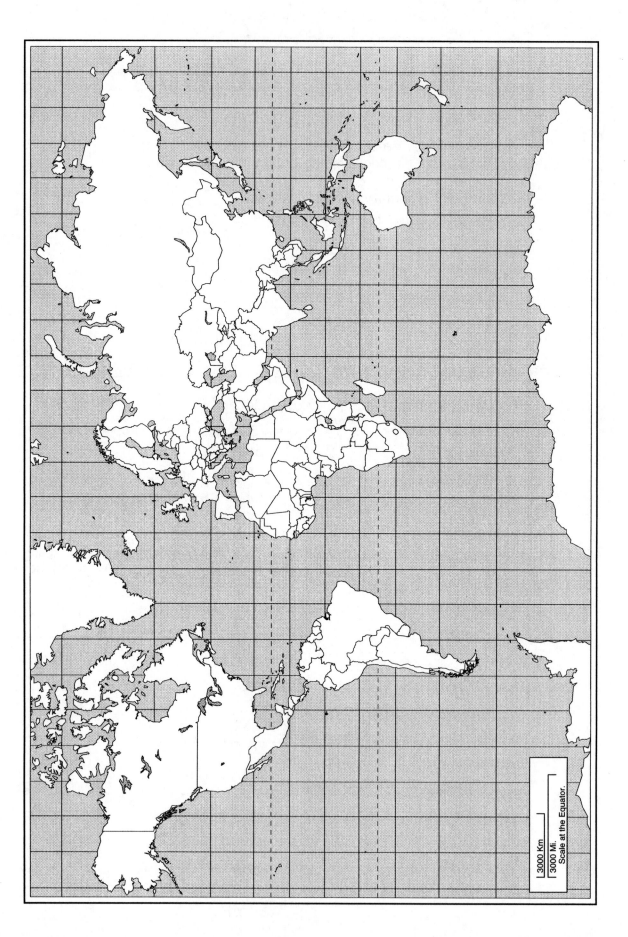

3000 Km

3000 Mi.

Scale at the Equator.

Looking for a Job

When you apply for a job, you have to fill out a job application that tells about you. Pretend you are applying for a job and complete this application.

Job Application for_____

Name _____
                Last   *First*   *Middle*

Address_____
                                      Street

      _____
            City   *State*   *Zip Code*

Telephone Number _____
                        Area Code

Birthdate _____
               Month   *Day*   *Year*

Work Experience _____

_____

_____

References _____

_____

_____

Why are you applying for this job? _____

_____

_____

_____

Name _____

Dress the Chicken and Trim the Steak

Amelia Bedelia dressed the chicken and trimmed the fat on the steak. Now it's your turn!

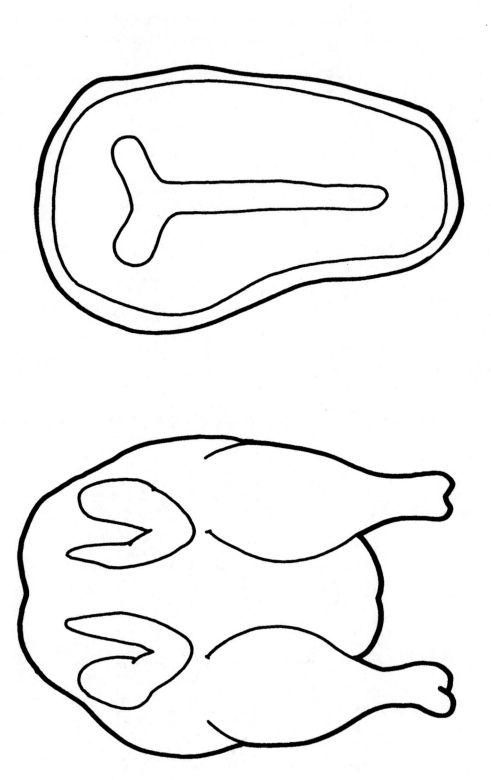

38

Name _____

A New Uniform for Amelia Bedelia

Uniforms are special clothes that people wear for their jobs. Write a list of people who wear uniforms on their jobs. When you are finished, draw a new uniform for Amelia Bedelia.

Amelia's New Uniform   ### People Who Wear Uniforms

_____

_____

_____

_____

_____

_____

_____

_____

_____

_____

_____

_____

Write a Song About Amelia Bedelia

Write a song about Amelia Bedelia to the tune of "Old MacDonald Had a Farm." Sing the song when you are finished.

Amelia Bedelia worked at _____

Amelia Bedelia worked at _____.

E-I-E-I-O!

And while at _____,

She liked to _____.

E-I-E-I-O!

With a _____ here,

And a _____ there,

Here a _____, there a _____,

Everywhere a _____.

Amelia Bedelia worked at _____.

E-I-E-I-O!

Amelia Bedelia worked at _____.

E-I-E-I-O!

And while at _____,

She liked to _____.

E-I-E-I-O!

With a _____ here,

And a _____ there,

Here a _____, there a _____,

Everywhere a _____.

Amelia Bedelia worked at _____,

E-I-E-I-O!

Name_____

Idiom Web

Read another book about Amelia Bedelia. Make a web using the idioms in the book.

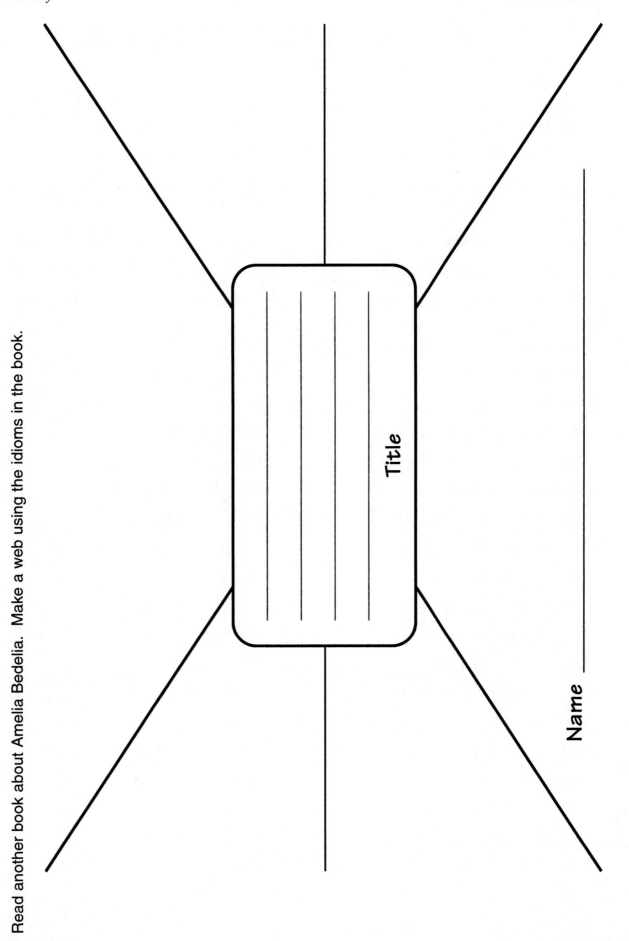

Title

Name

Master List of Idioms

Idioms	Meanings
1. In a pickle	Having a hard time
2. Butterflies in the stomach	Feelings of nervousness
3. Open a can of worms	Start trouble that will be hard to stop
4. White elephant	Something that's useless
5. Put your foot in your mouth	Say something you shouldn't have said
6. In one ear and out the other	Words you hear but don't pay attention to
7. Your eyes are bigger than your stomach	You take more food than you can eat.
8. Straight from the horse's mouth	Directly from the source
9. Give someone the cold shoulder	Ignore someone
10. A close shave	A close encounter with trouble
11. Crocodile tears	Fake tears
12. Get up on the wrong side of the bed	Wake up in a bad mood
13. Fly off the handle	Become upset quickly
14. Put on the dog	Try to be extra fancy
15. A chip off the old block	A child who is like his/her parents
16. Let the cat out of the bag	Reveal a secret
17. Get into everyone's hair	Keep bothering people
18. Sitting on top of the world	Feeling good about things
19. Going to the dogs	Falling apart
20. Raining cats and dogs	Raining very hard
21. Keep the wolf from the door	Work to pay the bills
22. For the birds	Silly or useless
23. Something is fishy here	Something is wrong
24. Don't bug me	Don't bother me
25. Don't rat on anyone	Don't tattle on anyone
26. Hold your horses	Wait
27. He/she is two-faced	He/she is dishonest

Master List of Idioms *(cont.)*

Idioms	Meanings
28. Face the music	Accept the consequences
29. Head in the clouds	Daydreaming or being unrealistic
30. Keep your head above water	Keep from falling behind
31. Pull the wool over someone's eyes	Fool someone
32. Eyes in the back of your head	Know everything that is happening
33. Watch your mouth	Be careful what you say
34. All ears	Listening to everything that is being said
35. A pain in the neck	Annoying
36. Have a green thumb	Able to make plants grow well
37. Walking on air	Light-hearted
38. Under the weather	Ill
39. Feeling blue	Feeling sad
40. A piece of cake	Easy
41. Going bananas	Going crazy
42. Spill the beans	Tell a secret
43. Put on your thinking cap	Use your head to solve a problem
44. A feather in your cap	Something to be proud of
45. The cat's got your tongue	You don't say anything because you're bashful
46. That's the way the cookie crumbles	That's the way things happen
47. Let's talk turkey	Let's talk seriously

> Now, add new idioms and their meanings to this list!

_____

_____

_____

Master Lists of "un" Words and Homonyms

A prefix is a syllable that is put at the beginning of a word to change its meaning. "Un" is a prefix that means "the opposite of."

1. unbend	11. unfasten	21. unlock	31. unsafe
2. unbroken	12. unfold	22. unlucky	32. unselfish
3. unbuckle	13. unfriendly	23. unnecessary	33. untidy
4. unclean	14. unhappy	24. unpack	34. untie
5. uncover	15. unhealthy	25. unpleasant	35. untrue
6. uncurl	16. unhook	26. unpopular	36. unused
7. uneven	17. unimportant	27. unready	37. unwelcome
8. unequal	18. unkind	28. unreal	38. unwilling
9. unfaded	19. unlawful	29. unripe	39. unwrap
10. unfair	20. unload	30. unroll	40. unwritten

Homonyms are words that sound alike, may be spelled alike or differently, and have different meanings.

1. ant • aunt	18. hi • high	35. pour • poor
2. ate • eight	19. hole • whole	36. prints • prince
3. bare • bear	20. I • eye	37. red • read
4. be • bee	21. made • maid	38. right • write
5. beat • beet	22. meat • meet	39. road • rode
6. blue • blew	23. new • knew	40. sale • sail
7. by • bye • buy	24. night • knight	41. sea • see
8. dear • deer	25. no • know	42. some • sum
9. die • dye	26. nose • knows	43. sew • so • sow
10. dock • Doc	27. oar • or	44. stair • stare
11. flour • flower	28. one • won	45. stake • steak
12. for • four • fore	29. our • hour	46. tail • tale
13. gym • Jim	30. pain • pane	47. to • too • two
14. hair • hare	31. pale • pail	48. toe • tow
15. hay • hey	32. peace • piece	49. weak • week
16. hear • here	33. pear • pare	50. weight • wait
17. heal • heel	34. plain • plane	

Bibliography

Other Amelia Bedelia Books

Books Written by Peggy Parish

Thank You, Amelia Bedelia. Harper, 1964.

Amelia Bedelia and the Surprise Shower. Harper, 1966.
Come Back, Amelia Bedelia. Harper, 1971.
Play Ball, Amelia Bedelia. Morrow, 1976.
Teach Us, Amelia Bedelia. Morrow, 1977.
Amelia Bedelia Helps Out. Greenwillow, 1979.
Amelia Bedelia and the Baby. Greenwillow, 1981.
Amelia Bedelia Goes Camping. Greenwillow, 1985.
Merry Christmas, Amelia Bedelia. Greenwillow, 1986.
Amelia Bedelia's Family Album. Greenwillow, 1988.

Books Written by Herman Parish

Good Driving, Amelia Bedelia. Greenwillow, 1995.

Related Fiction

Idioms
Terban, Marvin. *In a Pickle and Other Funny Idioms.* Clarion, 1983.
Terban, Marvin. *Mad as a Wet Hen! and Other Funny Idioms.* Clarion, 1987.

Homonyms
Gwynne, Fred. *A Chocolate Moose for Dinner.* Simon and Schuster, 1976.
Gwynne, Fred. *A Little Pigeon Toad.* Simon and Schuster, 1988.
Gwynne, Fred. *The King Who Rained.* Simon and Schuster, 1970.
Gwynne, Fred. *The Sixteen Hand Horse.* Simon and Schuster, 1980.
Terban, Marvin. *Eight Ate—A Feast of Homonym Riddles.* Clarion, 1982.

Related Nonfiction

Rice
Dooley, Norah. *Everyone Cooks Rice.* Carolrhoda, 1991.
Reller, Holly. *Grandfather's Dream.* Greenwillow, 1994.
Johnson, Sylvia. *Rice.* Lerner, 1985.

Audio-Visual Materials

SRA/McGraw-Hill
P.O. Box 543
Blacklick, OH, 43004-0543
1-800-843-8855
FAX 1-614-869-1877

Sound Filmstrips
Amelia Bedelia and the Baby
Amelia Bedelia and the Surprise Shower
Come Back, Amelia Bedelia
Good Work, Amelia Bedelia
Thank You, Amelia Bedelia

Read Along Audio Cassettes
Amelia Bedelia and the Baby
Amelia Bedelia and the Surprise Shower
Amelia Bedelia Helps Out
Charles Clark Co., Inc.
3043 Barrow Drive
Raleigh, NC, 27604
1-800-247-7009
FAX 919-954-7554

Books with Cassettes
Amelia Bedelia
Amelia Bedelia and the Surprise Shower
Come Back, Amelia Bedelia
Merry Christmas, Amelia Bedelia
Play Ball, Amelia Bedelia

Additional Ideas

Here are some ideas to help you get started with other Amelia Bedelia titles.

Thank You, Amelia Bedelia (1964)

1. Bring a jellyroll to class and discuss and taste it.
2. Brainstorm a homonym list. Pick a pair of homonyms, use them in sentences, and illustrate them. (Refer to the master list on page 44.)
3. Have a Class Shirt Day. Compare and contrast the shirts worn by students.
4. Extend the meaning of "pair" by pairing off students by similarities such as hair color, eye color, height, clothing, etc.
5. Design a shirt.

Amelia Bedelia and the Surprise Shower (1966)

1. Compare Amelia and her cousin, Alcolu. List how they are alike and different.
2. Research different kinds of scales. Weigh different items in the classroom.
3. Use the stick puppets on pages 16 and 17 to dramatize scenes from the book.
4. Make a collage from cut-paper flowers.
5. Complete the Amelia and Alcolu acrostics on page 23.
6. Write an acrostic using your name and your cousin's name. If you don't have a cousin, make up a name!
7. Make chocolate cupcakes.

Come Back, Amelia Bedelia (1971)

1. Invite a beautician, doctor, tailor (seamstress), and/or office manager to share their careers with the class.
2. Gather "Help Wanted" ads from the newspaper. Read, discuss, and analyze the jobs.
3. Complete the Looking for a Job activity on page 37.
4. Choose a job and make a "Help Wanted" sign, including requirements for the position.
5. Research skills needed to be a beautician, doctor, tailor (seamstress), and office manager.

Play Ball, Amelia Bedelia (1972)

1. Learn the rules of baseball. Play a modified version, using plastic or sponge bats and balls.
2. Design a baseball uniform, including a new team name.
3. Draw a diagram of a baseball field and label the positions.
4. Review and discuss baseball terms in the book, such as pop fly, steal bases, etc.
5. Brainstorm a list using numbers in baseball: 3 outs, 3 strikes, 4 balls, 9 innings, shirt numbers, 9 players on the field, etc.

Additional Ideas (cont.)

Good Work, Amelia Bedelia (1976)

1. Make a word search using the words from the book.
2. Prepare bread using yeast. Record procedure and results on page 33.
3. Make patchwork squares.
4. Complete the Likes and Dislikes activity on page 34.

Teach Us, Amelia Bedelia (1977)

1. Complete Telephone Tricks on page 30.
2. Create a "roll" of the students in the class in ABC order.
3. Write a new song about Amelia Bedelia on page 40.
4. Plant flowers and vegetables and record growth.
5. Make caramel apples.

Amelia Bedelia Helps Out (1979)

1. Write a story about your favorite aunt (real or imagined).
2. Web the idioms in the story, using page 41.
3. Brainstorm a list of "un" words. Refer to the master list on page 44.
4. Plant beans or grass seeds. Then observe and record their growth on page 33.
5. Write math story problems using items in the story, such as grass seeds, beans, weeds, bugs, etc.

Amelia Bedelia and the Baby (1981)

1. List a babysitter's responsibilities.
2. Write a recipe for strawberry tarts on page 22.
3. Design a new toy for a baby.
4. Pretend Amelia Bedelia is your babysitter. Write about your experiences.

Amelia Bedelia Goes Camping (1985)

1. List the skills one needs when camping.
2. Visit a camp in your area.
3. Research different kinds of fish you can eat.
4. Look up the word "pitch" in the dictionary. Discuss the different meanings.

Merry Christmas, Amelia Bedelia (1986)

1. Write a poem using each month of the year.
2. Brainstorm Christmas customs.
3. Make an ABC book of Christmas words.
4. Create a Christmas gift to give to Amelia Bedelia.
5. Experiment with popcorn. Measure one cup, and then pop and measure again. Use page 33 to record results.
6. Make popcorn balls.

Amelia Bedelia's Family Album (1988)

1. Write a book about your family.
2. Amelia Bedelia has worn the same uniform in all the books so far. Use page 39 to design a new uniform for her.
3. List the careers of Amelia's relatives.
4. Pick your favorite relative and write a story about him/her.
5. Invite family members to visit the class and share their careers.

Good Driving, Amelia Bedelia (1995)

1. Use road maps to locate towns, cities, highways, etc.
2. Pretend you can drive. Write a story about where you would go.
3. Use the stick puppets on pages 16 and 17 to act out this story.
4. List and discuss homonyms used in the book.
5. Research how one obtains a driver's license.

Reading Record

Use this record to keep track of the Amelia Bedelia books you read. After you read each book, write your name next to the book's title. Then color a picture to go with that book and clip it to the back of this title page.

	Name	**Date**
Thank You, Amelia Bedelia	_____	_____
Amelia Bedelia and the Surprise Shower	_____	_____
Come Back, Amelia Bedelia	_____	_____
Play Ball, Amelia Bedelia	_____	_____
Good Work, Amelia Bedelia	_____	_____
Teach Us, Amelia Bedelia	_____	_____
Amelia Bedelia Helps Out	_____	_____
Amelia Bedelia and the Baby	_____	_____
Amelia Bedelia Goes Camping	_____	_____
Merry Christmas, Amelia Bedelia	_____	_____
Amelia Bedelia's Family Album	_____	_____
Good Driving, Amelia Bedelia	_____	_____